KATHY STINSON

The Girl Who Loved Giraffes

AND BECAME THE WORLD'S FIRST GIRAFFOLOGIST

ILLUSTRATED BY

FRANÇOIS THISDALE

Fitzhenry & Whiteside

Published in Canada by Fitzhenry & Whiteside
195 Allstate Parkway, Markham, ON L3R 4T8

Published in the United States by Fitzhenry & Whiteside,
311 Washington Street, Brighton, MA 02135

2 4 6 5 3 1

Fitzhenry & Whiteside acknowledges with thanks the Canada Council for the Arts and the Ontario Arts Council for their support of our publishing program. We acknowledge the financial support of the Government of Canada through the Canada Book Fund (CBF) for our publishing activities.

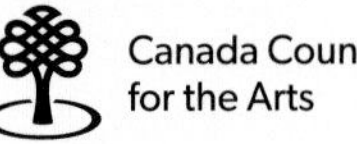

Library and Archives Canada Cataloguing in Publication
Title: The girl who loved giraffes and became the world's first giraffologist / written by Kathy Stinson ; illustrated by François Thisdale.
Names: Stinson, Kathy, author. | Thisdale, François, 1964- illustrator.
Identifiers: ISBN 9781554555406 (hardcover)
Subjects: LCSH: Dagg, Anne Innis—Juvenile literature. | LCSH: Zoologists—Canada—Biography—Juvenile iterature. | LCSH: Women zoologists—Canada—Biography—Juvenile literature. | LCSH: Giraffe—Africa—Juvenile literature.
Classification: LCC QL31.D34 S75 2021 | DDC j590.92—dc23

Publisher Cataloging-in-Publication Data (U.S.)
Names: Stinson, Kathy, author. | Thisdale, François, 1964-, illustrator.
Title: The Girl Who Loved Giraffes : and Became the World's First Giraffologist / by Kathy Stinson ; illustrated by François Thisdale.
Description: Markham, Ontario : Fitzhenry & Whiteside, 2021.| Summary: "A gem of a book that captures the dramatic story of Anne's life, the majestic beauty of giraffes, and fascinating facts about this most intriguing and magnificent creature. Anne Innis Dagg herself is thrilled that the book will cause young readers to fall in love with giraffes as she did, and bring their attention to the cause dearest to her heart, that of giraffe conservation" – Provided by publisher.
Identifiers: ISBN 978-1-55455-540-6 (paperback)
Subjects: LCSH Giraffe –Juvenile literature. | Dagg, Anne Innis – Juvenile literature. | Biologists – Biography – Juvenile literature. | BISAC: JUVENILE NONFICTION / Animals / Giraffes. | JUVENILE NONFICTION / Biography & Autobiography / Women.
Classification: LCC QL737.U56 |DDC 599.638 – dc23

Edited by Beverley Brenna
Design by Kong Njo

Printed in Hong Kong by Sheck Wah Tong Printing

fitzhenry.ca

Cover image of giraffes adapted from photo by Dr. Francois Deacon. Used with his permission and that of the filmmakers of "*The Woman Who Loves Giraffes*" documentary.

To giraffe conservationists, past, present, and future, with thanks

—K.S.

To Jean-Pierre, my dear father-in-law, 1930-2020

—F.T.

“We must work together,
each of us doing what we can,
to make sure we will always have
these extraordinary animals in the wild.”

“I never thought of myself as a woman.
I just thought I was a person.”

—Anne Innis Dagg

CONTENTS

"No Girls Allowed" #1	7
Anne's First Giraffe	8
Anne Makes A Plan	10
Getting Ready for Africa	12
"No Girls Allowed" #2	15
A Long Journey	16
"A Very Determined Young Woman"	18
Almost There	21
One More Problem	22
Anne's First Wild Giraffe	24
Dozens of Giraffes	26
And More Giraffes	28
A Dead Giraffe	30
Giraffes, Fierce and Friendly	32
Another Giraffe Question	34
Giraffe Babies	35
Galloping Free	36
How Giraffes Move	38
"No Girls Allowed" #3	40
What Next?	42
"Our Hero"	44
New Information About Giraffes	45
Shocking News	47
Fighting for Giraffe Survival	48
Anne's Love of Giraffe Continues	51
Author's Note	52
Glossary	54
Find Out More	55
Acknowledgments	56

“No Girls Allowed” #1

Long ago, far from the hot continent where giraffes live, a baby girl was born. Her parents named her Anne.

Soon Anne wanted to join the games her brothers were playing. They laughed and shouted, “No girls allowed.”

“Not fair,” Anne grumbled.

Anne’s father, Harold Innis, was a professor. Her mother, Mary Quayle Innis, was a writer.

Anne's First Giraffe

At the zoo, Anne saw large animals in small pens. That didn't seem fair either.

She gazed up at the tallest animal by far.

The giraffe peered down. It looked right at her.

The hair on the back of Anne's neck tickled.

"Aren't you peculiar!" she whispered. "I want to know all about you."

Giraffes are the tallest animals in the world. An adult male weighs as much as two grand pianos. Yet a giraffe has only seven vertebrae in its neck, the same number humans do. Vertebrae are the bones of the neck and back.

Anne Makes A Plan

Anne loved reading, especially about animals. She used index cards to keep track of every book she read.

She searched long and hard for books about giraffes, but there weren't any.

In an encyclopedia, she learned:

> Outside of zoos, giraffes live only in the open woods and grasslands of Africa.

"I have to go to Africa," Anne said, "where giraffes roam free and I can learn all about them."

Her mother said, "You'd better finish school first."

Her friend said, "Won't that cost a lot of money?"

Her brother said, "That's far for a girl. You'll be too scared to go."

Africa is the second largest of the seven continents. Among the African countries where giraffes live are Kenya, Niger, Uganda, Namibia, Zambia, Tanzania, and South Africa.

Getting Ready for Africa

Anne saved all her allowance. When she was old enough, she got a summer job.

At university, her good marks in Biology earned her a gold medal and a prize of money to add to her savings.

When all she needed was a place in Africa to stay, Anne wrote thirteen letters to African wildlife organizations and universities, telling them her plan to live near giraffes and study them.

She waited eagerly for answers.

Biology is the science of living things.

There was no such thing as e-mail in the 1950s. People had to type letters one at a time on a typewriter, put them in envelopes, and take them to the post office to be mailed. It could take days and even weeks for a letter to be delivered, and days or weeks more for a reply to come back.

UNDERWOOD
STANDARD TYPEWRITER

AIR MAIL

"No Girls Allowed" #2

All the answers said there was nowhere in Africa for Anne to stay. One letter even said:

> Dear Miss Innis,
> Travelling alone to study giraffes is not something a young woman should do.

Anne ripped that letter into tiny pieces and pounded out another. This time, instead of signing it *Anne Innis*, she signed *A. Innis*. With luck, the person getting *this* letter would think *A* stood for *Allan* or *Albert*. Sure enough . . .

> Dear Mr. Innis,
> You can stay at my ranch and bunk with the cowhands.
>
> Yours truly,
> Alexander Matthew

"I'm going!" Anne cheered. "At last I'm going to Africa to learn about giraffes!"

"But Mr. Matthew thinks you're a man," her mother said.

"I'll sort that out later!" said Anne.

In the 1950s, most women were expected to marry and take care of their homes and families while their husbands went out to work. Women might work outside the home for a while, but usually only until they got married.

A Long Journey

Anne boarded a train in Toronto. From Montreal she sailed on an enormous ship.

From England she sent another letter.

> Dear Mr. Matthew,
> I am super excited to be on
> my way to seeing giraffes.
>
> Yours ecstatically,
> Anne Innis

Then she was off to South Africa!

Soon after *that* ship landed—*two months* after she had left home—Anne found out that Mr. Matthew's ranch was still *a thousand miles* away. No trains or buses went anywhere near it.

So Anne bought herself an old car. She named it *Camelo,* short for the scientific name for giraffes.

Canadians and South Africans didn't think in metric until the 1970s. 1000 miles is about 1500 kilometers, roughly the distance between Chilliwack, British Columbia and Moose Jaw, Saskatchewan, or between Springfield, Massachusetts and Chicago, Illinois. A long way, however it's measured.

The scientific name for giraffe is *Camelopardalis* (Camel-oh-par-DAL-is). People used to think a giraffe was part camel because of its size and part leopard because of its markings.

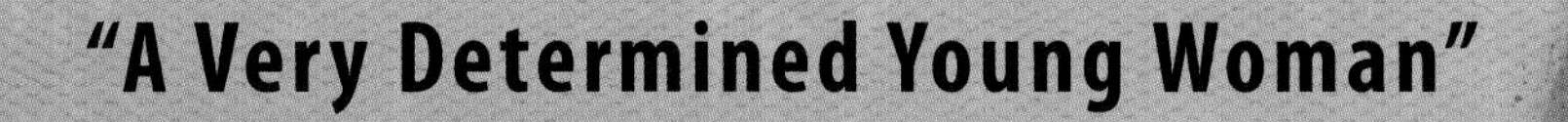

"A Very Determined Young Woman"

As Anne prepared for the last leg of her journey, she received a letter.

Dear Anne,
I'm sorry, but I thought you were a man. I'm afraid you can't stay at my ranch after all.

Sincerely,
Alexander Matthew

He could *not* turn her away *now!* He *couldn't!*

Dear Mr. Matthew,
I have wanted to study giraffes my whole life! I have come so far and have nowhere else to go! Please may I come? Please? I can sleep in a tent!

Yours desperately,
Anne

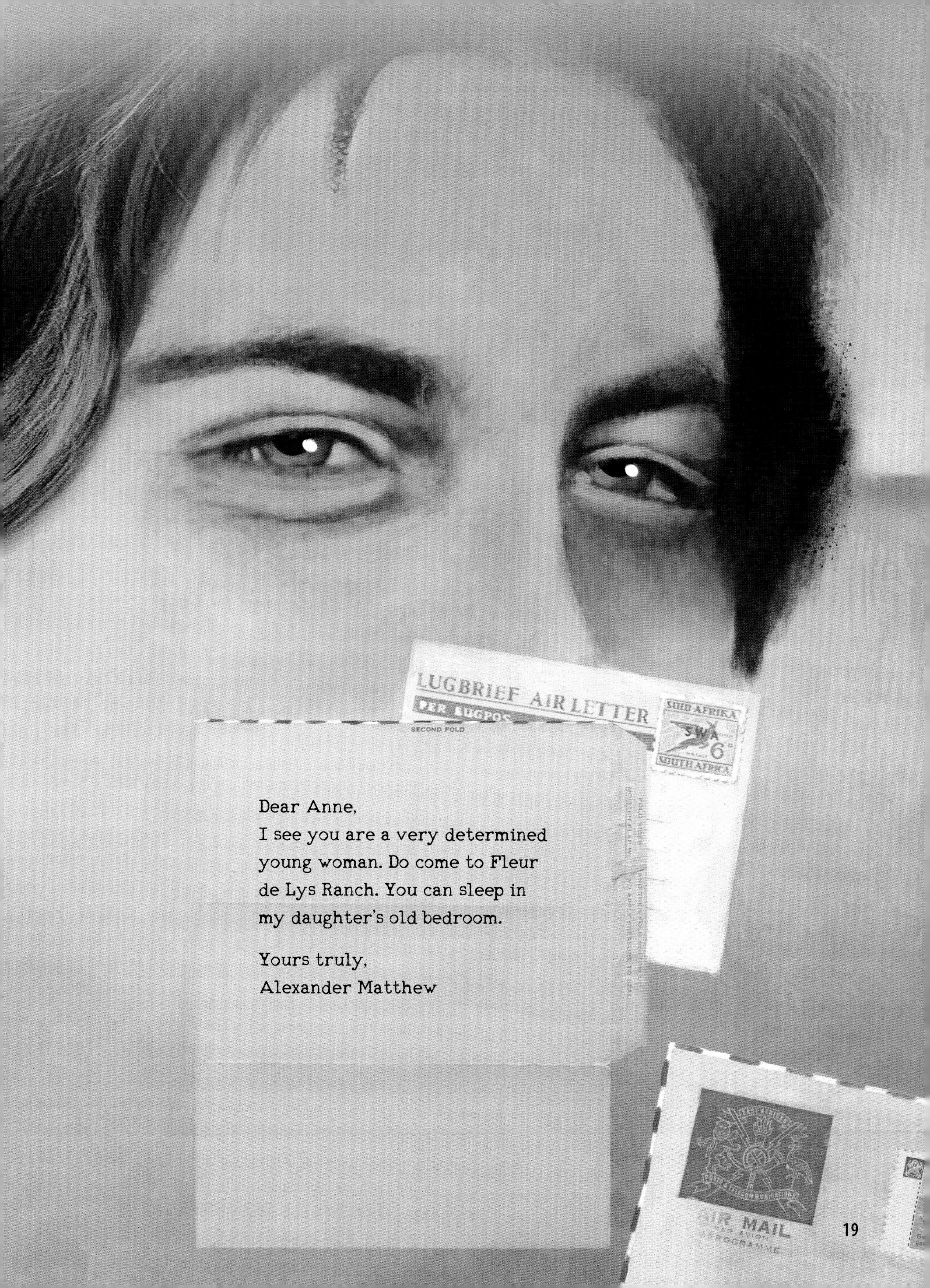
Dear Anne,
I see you are a very determined young woman. Do come to Fleur de Lys Ranch. You can sleep in my daughter's old bedroom.

Yours truly,
Alexander Matthew

Fleur de Lys
Nelspruit
SOUTH AFRICA
Molopolole
Petersburg
Leydsdorp
Nylstroom
Lydenburg
Rustenburg
Pretoria
Johannesburg
Potchefstroom
Vryburg
Mamusa
Harrismith
Bloemfontein
NATAL
Pietermaritzburg
Stanger
Fauresmith
Smithfield
Colesberg
Burghersdorp
Griqua Land
East
Pondo
Ipolela
Utrecht
Greytown
NORTH EASTERN
King Williams Town
East London
SOUTH AFRICA
English Miles

Almost There

For two full days and into the night, Anne drove. The air was hot. It smelled wonderfully unlike anywhere she had ever been. And she was *so close* now to where there would be *giraffes!* She would be free to study them for a whole year!

One More Problem

Almost at Fleur de Lys, Anne's car shuddered and sputtered to a stop. It refused to start.

The night was pitch dark. There were no streetlights, no moon, and no way to let anyone know her predicament.

She would have to walk the rest of the way.

Slowly Anne got out of the car, her heart pounding in terror.

Step by step, she inched along the road toward the ranch.

At every bump in the dirt, she gasped.

At every rustle in the bushes, she jumped.

If she were to be eaten by a lion or bitten by a deadly snake—without ever having seen a single giraffe here—she would be *really mad!*

Then—

Headlights!

The driver leaned out his window. "You must be the Canadian girl."

Anne scrambled into the truck.

Finally, her adventure with giraffes was about to begin!

Anne's First Wild Giraffe

Anne parked near a waterhole. Soon a giraffe sauntered near, its long neck reaching high into the trees! And then another!

Out in the open, they looked *so majestic*. Anne's whole body tingled. How could any animal be so *enormous*—and *so elegant?*

At the edge of the water, one giraffe stretched its long legs wide apart and bent down to drink. Then quickly—so *very* quickly!—it flung its head back up.

How could it lift its head so far and so fast without fainting?

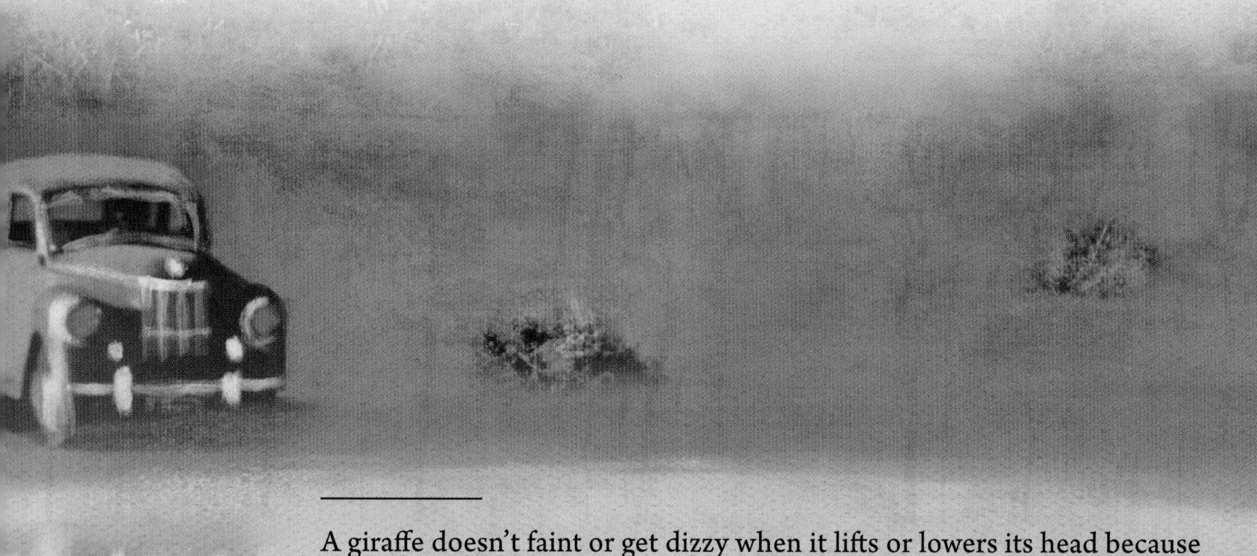

A giraffe doesn't faint or get dizzy when it lifts or lowers its head because inside the many tiny blood vessels near its brain are little flaps that open and close. These flaps prevent blood from flowing up or down its neck too quickly.

Lions, especially in groups, can easily attack a giraffe when it's drinking. So one giraffe often stands guard while another drinks. A giraffe's legs are so powerful it can kill a lion with one kick. Its hooves are the size of dinner plates.

SUID-AFRIKA

Dozens of Giraffes

Every morning Anne hurried out of bed, eager for the chance to be with giraffes. As a scientist, she wrote down everything she observed. She made charts and drawings and took photographs too.

Often the giraffes were walking from tree to tree, pulling leaves from the branches with their long, dark tongues. Didn't the thorns of acacia trees hurt their mouths?

Digital cameras hadn't yet been invented in 1956. Images were captured on film that had to be loaded into the camera. A roll of film held just 24 or 36 photos. When the roll was full, it was taken to where the photos could be printed. It could be days or even weeks before a person saw the photos they had taken.

Giraffes eat 90 different kinds of leaves, most often from acacia trees. The leaves one giraffe eats in a day weigh as much as a ten-year-old human and contain so much water that the giraffe only needs to drink every few days, or even every few weeks.

And More Giraffes

Anne soon got to know some of the giraffes well enough to name them—Pom-Pom because the hair on her ossicones was so long, Star because of the shape of his markings.

For Anne, even watching giraffes at rest was thrilling.

Once, after sitting in Camelo for hours, she got out to stretch. The giraffes turned and stared at her. Then one snorted and they all walked away.

Anne didn't want anything she did to change how the animals behaved naturally, so after that she stayed inside Camelo to study them, no matter how uncomfortable she was.

Each giraffe's markings are as unique as a person's fingerprints.

Ossicones are what many people would call horns.

All young giraffes and adult females have hair on their ossicones.

Adult giraffes take a few very short sleeps each day, usually standing. They are awkward and slow getting up, so lying down is dangerous when lions are nearby.

A Dead Giraffe

One day, a worker shouted, "A giraffe has been shot out near the road!"

Anne felt as if her heart might break in two. But, she told herself, she was a zoologist, and here was a chance to learn things she couldn't learn from a living giraffe.

Dear Mom,
Today workers were cutting up a dead giraffe for its meat and you won't believe what I did. I strung the intestines on a clothesline so I could measure them. They were 256 feet long!

I may also have found out why thorns don't seem to bother giraffes when they're eating. The skin on their lips is really thick and covered with bristly hair. The tongue—which is almost as long as my arm—is rough and covered with thick, sticky saliva.

I will be very happy to be studying *live* giraffes again tomorrow.

Love, Anne

A zoologist is someone who studies the science of animals.

A giraffe's intestines are about 76 meters (250 feet) long—not quite as long as a football field. Intestines are the organs food passes through after leaving the stomach.

Saliva is the liquid in a person's or animal's mouth.

Giraffes, Fierce and Friendly

THUNK! THUD! THUNK!

Anne drove quickly toward the sound.

Two male giraffes were swinging their powerful necks and bashing each other, hard, with their heads.

Anne cringed with each blow. But amazingly, neither giraffe got hurt.

Other times Anne saw male giraffes rubbing their necks together in a way that looked very friendly.

The hair on giraffe ossicones gets worn off when they spar. And sometimes giraffes do get hurt when sparring. The winner of the fight gets to mate with the female he chooses. A male giraffe can tell if a female is ready to mate by sniffing or tasting her urine. To mate means to come together to produce young.

Another Giraffe Question

Even after studying giraffes for months, Anne never tired of watching them ambling among the trees or occasionally running across open spaces.

She told Mr. Matthew, "I keep trying to figure out how they manage to move without tripping over their long legs."

"Would you like to borrow my movie camera and film them?" he asked.

Anne wished she had the movie camera with her the day she saw giraffes mating. But film was expensive. She could afford only so much.

Sadly, the baby would not be born until after Anne was back in Canada.

Packing her suitcase for the journey home, Anne tried not to cry. She might never get back to Africa again! How she would miss being among all the giraffes that roamed freely at Fleur de Lys.

A giraffe is pregnant for fifteen months. She usually has only one baby at a time. A giraffe mother gives birth to her baby standing up. The thump when the baby hits the ground helps it start breathing. A baby giraffe can stand when it's only one hour old, and sometimes sooner. It already weighs as much a full-grown man and is just as tall.

Galloping Free

Across the open grassland, Anne spotted what she knew would be her last group of giraffes. One started to gallop. The others followed.

Watching them galloping together, tails curled over their backs, their mighty necks moving back and forth with each step, Anne felt as if her heart might fly right out of her chest—as if *she* were galloping too . . . *galloping, galloping, wild and free!*

How Giraffes Move

Back in Canada, Anne watched giraffes moving powerfully across the screen. She watched the film over and over again, spellbound.

Then she replayed the film as a scientist, pausing it frame by frame, and tracing the giraffes' legs.

When writing about giraffes for other scientists, and speaking to university students, Anne used her drawings to help explain exactly how giraffes move without tripping.

When a giraffe is walking, its front and back leg on one side move forward, followed by the front and back leg on the other side. When a giraffe is running, its two front legs move first, and then the back.

"No Girls Allowed" #3

Students loved hearing Anne share her passion for animals, and Anne loved her students. She decided to become a full-time zoology professor.

But men doing the hiring at universities near Anne's home said she wasn't qualified for the job.

"Not qualified?" Anne furiously set the table for supper. "I have a *PhD in Animal Behaviour!* The best science magazines *in the world* have published my discoveries!"

Another university said they wouldn't hire Anne because she was married.

What?!

For seven years Anne wrote letters trying to convince someone she had been treated unfairly. She even went to court.

The judge said the universities had done nothing wrong.

Zoology is the science of animals.

A PhD is the highest university degree a person can get.

What Next?

Anne threw herself into writing about how women should be free to do the kinds of work they want.

With another scientist, she wrote a book called *The Giraffe*, jam-packed with information.

She found another way to work with students—giving them ideas about how to go about their research and how to improve their writing. She did this job for many years, and continued writing about women's rights, animals, and other things she cared deeply about.

More than fifty years after leaving her giraffes galloping across the open grassland of Africa, Anne opened an e-mail.

> We are having our first ever conference
> for people who work with giraffes.
> We hope you will come as our guest.

Anne felt a tingle of excitement.

> Thank you for inviting me to your conference.
> I have not worked with giraffes in a very long time,
> but I would like to come.

By the 1970s, more women in North America were working outside the home than had been twenty years earlier, but they were often paid less than men. In 1977 it became illegal in Canada to discriminate against women, but women are still fighting for the right to do certain jobs and the right for equal pay.

To discriminate against someone means to treat them unfairly because of who they are.

Giraffe

"Our Hero"

From all over the world giraffologists came—giraffe scientists, giraffe researchers, and giraffe keepers. They had all—for decades—been reading Anne's book!

"You're a pioneer!" they told her. "Our hero!"

"Your book made me want to study giraffes too."

"That is *super!*" Anne said. Being among other people who cared about giraffes—and her giraffe work—she couldn't stop beaming.

"Giraffologist" is a word that Alexander Matthew made up in one of his letters to Anne after her return to Canada. Since an "ologist" is someone who studies a certain subject, a person who specializes in the study of giraffes is a "giraffologist."

New Information About Giraffes

The other giraffologists—men and women—were keen to share with Anne all they had been learning, and she was keen to hear it.

Mother giraffes will sometimes leave their babies together with one mother—a babysitter—while the others go off to eat.

Giraffes make sounds so low that humans can't hear them. They use them to communicate with each other, even from quite far away.

In small doses, oils in a giraffe's skin smell like jasmine and orange blossoms.

Shocking News

But giraffes in Africa were in trouble. Big trouble.

They were becoming an endangered species.

"If we don't do enough to help them," a young giraffe researcher said, "it's possible that some day there will be no giraffes living in the wild at all."

Anne shuddered. "We cannot let that happen."

Highways and cities take over areas where giraffes live. They're like a sign saying "No Giraffes Allowed."

Climate change brings long periods without rain. Trees and crops suffer, so giraffes and people are hungry.

People hunt giraffes for their meat, and for their skin, bones, or tails.

On lists kept by The International Union for the Conservation of Nature, "endangered" is only two steps away from "extinct in the wild." Extinct means no longer in existence.

Fighting for Giraffe Survival

Back to Africa Anne went, to see what conservationists were doing to help save the giraffes.

They were hiring rangers and guards to protect giraffes from hunters.

They were teaching villagers ways to make money so they wouldn't need to sell giraffe skins and tails.

They were moving giraffes from the most dangerous areas to natural sanctuaries for their protection.

They were taking school children to see giraffes in the wild.

They were urging governments to make decisions about the environment that would help protect all animals and their habitats.

They were encouraging people everywhere to help spread the word about the trouble giraffes were in.

A conservationist works to protect and preserve wildlife and the environment.

Anne's Love of Giraffe Continues

By the waterhole where she had seen her first wild giraffe, Anne stood very still.

Eventually a giraffe sauntered near.

Anne smiled. It was just so *magnificent*! It might even be Pom-Pom's great-granddaughter or great-great-granddaughter!

She focused her camera.

The giraffe turned and looked right at her.

The hair on the back of Anne's neck tickled.

"You are extraordinary," she whispered, "and I will do all I can to help save you."

AUTHOR'S NOTE

When Anne went to Africa in 1956 at the age of twenty-three, she didn't know she was a pioneer in the scientific study of an animal's behaviour in the wild. She didn't know she would one day become the world's leading expert on giraffes either. But by pursuing her passion with courage and determination, she did.

Many years later, Anne Innis Dagg has received awards for "excellence in science" and "lifetime achievement." Her work has been included in museum exhibits like "Courage and Passion: Canadian Women in Natural Science"—about "women who broke barriers to pursue their passion for science." Someone has even made a movie about her—*The Woman Who Loves Giraffes*. When Anne is introduced to audiences after they have watched it, she always gets a standing ovation.

The honours are well-deserved and Anne enjoys the attention. But she cares most of all about giraffes. When the film-maker, Alison Reid, approached her, wanting to make her film, Anne said, "Make it about giraffes so everyone who sees it will love them and want to help save them." When Anne's 2016 book, *5 Giraffes*, won a prize for "Best in Canadian Science Writing," she donated all the prize money to giraffe conservation. In 2020 she helped establish the Anne Innis Dagg Foundation to further support giraffe conservation work.

Now in her eighties, Anne still loves learning what giraffologists are discovering—things like if a baby giraffe dies, its mother will stay with it for hours, sometimes days, and other females will keep her company. There is still much to learn and Anne hopes some of the young people reading about her and giraffes will themselves decide to become giraffologists, doing their own research and working to save these magnificent animals.

Anne still cares about girls and women getting to do jobs they're keen to do, free of discrimination, too. In 2017 she took part in the Women's March in Washington, joining millions around the world marching to say to governments that women's rights are human rights. She is pleased to see young people today standing up for what they believe in.

In 2019 one of the universities that didn't hire Anne granted her an honorary degree. Another apologized for having treated her and other women unfairly, announced a scholarship for female science students in Anne's name, and made a generous donation to giraffe conservation.

In 1985 there were between 151,000 and 163,000 giraffes living in the wild. In 2020 there were fewer than 80,000.

But there is hope. Governments of 106 countries voted recently to put giraffes on the list of animals to be protected from the illegal selling of the parts or items made from their parts. And giraffe conservation work continues.

A portion of the royalties for this book will be donated to giraffe conservation in the hope that when today's young readers want to visit giraffes in the wild, giraffes will still be there—galloping free.

Photo Credits

Opposite page: The photo of Anne in the car from which she studied giraffes in 1956-57 was taken by Alexander Matthew. Used with the permission of Anne Innis Dagg.

Top: The photo of Anne with the children at the Eco Children School in South Africa was taken by Alison Reid. Used with the permission of Alison Reid, Free Spirit Films.

GLOSSARY

biology—the science of living things

Camelopardalis—the scientific name for giraffe, pronounced Camel-oh-par-DAL-is

conservationist—a person who works to protect and preserve wildlife and the environment

discriminate—treat someone unfairly because of who they are

endangered—in danger of becoming extinct

extinct—no longer in existence

giraffologist—a scientist who specializes in the study of giraffes, or a person who works with giraffes in other ways

intestines—organs that food passes through after leaving the stomach

mate—come together to produce young

ossicones—what many people would call horns

PhD—Doctor of Philosophy; the highest university degree a person can get

saliva—the liquid in a person's or animal's mouth

vertebrae—bones of the neck and back

zoology—the science of animals

FIND OUT MORE

Books by Anne Innis Dagg

5 Giraffes
(Fitzhenry & Whiteside 2016)

Giraffe: Biology, Behaviour and Conservation
(Cambridge University Press 2013)

Pursuing Giraffe: A 1950s adventure
(Wilfrid Laurier University Press 2006)

Smitten by Giraffe: My Life as a Citizen Scientist
(McGill University Press 2016)

The Woman Who Loves Giraffes
(Free Spirit Films 2018)
thewomanwholovesgiraffes.com

Giraffes: The Forgotten Giants
(CBC TV The Nature of Things 2015)
cbc.ca/natureofthings/episodes/
giraffes-the-forgotten-giants

Wild Journey: The Anne Innis Story
(CBC Radio Ideas 2013)
cbc.ca/player/play/2433567168

Anne Innis Dagg (AID) Foundation
anneinnisdaggfoundation.org

ACKNOWLEDGMENTS

What a privilege and treat it has been, getting to know the extraordinary Anne Innis Dagg during the course of working on this book. She read many versions of the manuscript, firmly correcting my misunderstanding of certain facts and always generous with her trademark "Super!" when I got things right. We shared lots of laughs and walks and I'm grateful for the friendship that developed between us after she agreed to let me write her story. Thank you, Anne.

I began learning about Anne and her work when I attended a screening of "The Woman Who Loves Giraffes" at the Bookshelf Cinema in Guelph. By the time the film had ended and I'd heard Anne speak as a guest panelist following the screening, I knew I had to write a book for kids about this amazing woman and the magnificent animals she has loved her whole life. Thank you, Alison Reid and the rest of the crew at Free Spirit Films for your jaw-droppingly gorgeous and emotionally captivating documentary, and thank you, Peter Henderson, for choosing it for the Bookshelf's Secret Cinema series.

Thanks also to Anne's daughter, Mary Dagg, and Anne's friend since childhood, Mary Williamson, who along with Anne shared stories and resources with me. I'm sorry I wasn't able to include more of them in the book. Also to Anne's son, Ian, who on World Giraffe Day at the Toronto Zoo in 2019 helped make me and my partner, Peter Carver, feel like part of the family.

I am more than grateful to Peter for giving me the nudge I needed to approach Anne at the Bookshelf that day. The road from book idea to publication can be as bumpy and twisty as the road Anne took through South Africa in 1956, and Peter's support in navigating the hazards on this one was invaluable.

Input and encouragement from others along the way, including Richard Dionne, has meant a lot to me too. It was his decision to take on this project and who suggested François Thisdale as the ideal illustrator for it. I have also benefited from support of one kind or another from friends and family members too numerous to name. I adore you all.

I acknowledge the caring and enthusiastic efforts of my editor, Beverley Brenna (I thought I was a stickler for precision of language and facts!); the book's designer, Kong Njo, who rose beautifully to the challenges this project presented; and the incomparable François Thisdale, as cheerful and easy-going a team member as he is a talented artist.

One last acknowledgement to John and Veda Carver, who in 1998 took me to Kruger National Park, where I first saw giraffes in their natural habitat—a very different experience from seeing them in a zoo. This book has been an adventure that, although I didn't know it at the time, began there.

ALAND
Palapye
Shoshong
Dakveed
Limpopo
Country
Boatlanams
ECTORATE
Molopolole
Kolobeng
Monope
Kanye
s Country
Marabastad
Petersburg
Leydsdorp
Valdezia
Hanglip
Water Berge
Nylstroom
SOUTH AFRICA
Breyer
Lydenburg
Pretoria
Middelburg
Johannesburg
New Scotland
Heidelberg
Potchefstroom
STELLA LAND
Vryburg
Heilbron
Vaal R.
Standerton
Charlestown
Kronstad
Utrecht
ORANGE FREE STATE
Harrismith
Ladysmith
Kimberley
Winburg
Greytown
Hope Town
Belmont
NATAL
Pietermaritzburg
Estcourt
SOUTH AFRICA